BEYOND

THE HEADLINES

MEDIA RELATIONS ABC'S FOR

21ST CENTURY PUBLIC SAFETY

AGENCIES

Wayne A. Delk

ISBN: 9798857949191

To my brothers and sisters of public safety:

In the quiet moments before dawn, in the chaos of emergencies, and in the countless hours of preparation and training, you stand unwavering, dedicated to the safety and well-being of our communities. I've walked in those boots, felt the weight of the badge, and understand the profound responsibility it carries. Our stories are not just headlines; they are a testament to our commitment, sacrifices, and the bonds we share. This book is a bridge between our world and the public we serve, ensuring that those of us in the business of telling our narratives do so with the authenticity, respect, and honor they deserve.

CONTENTS

Public Relations – The professional maintenance of a favorable public image by a company or other organization or a famous person; the state of the relationship between a company or other organization or a famous person and the public.

Oxford English Dictionary

What is public relations? And how does it tie into media relations and the work of the public information officer? The textbook definition is one thing, and it describes in the blandest of terms what public relations means to those who work at it. But what is it to those of us who are venturing into the muck of the public realm? What is it to you who are braving the deep waters of the feeding sharks of public opinion? If you bring blood into the water, the sharks will surely attack and a feeding frenzy will ensue. Media are all about the blood. If it bleeds, it leads.

And the sources for the blood are more readily available today than ever. Those things so easily hidden in the past ought not be tried today, for the ever watchful eye of the public is almost everywhere, and the voice of the public is but a click and share away from the world. Today's relationship with the public is an almost instantaneous one; from celebrities to corporate giants to small startups to public agencies. We can all reach out and connect with any and everyone at almost any time we want. But so too can the missteps, misspeaks, and mishaps find their way to the public. And if we aren't quick to own them and address them, they can take on a life of their own.

According the Public Relations Society of America, media relations is but one part of a much larger world of public relations. And media relations, though the initial work of newly coined public information officers in the public safety realm some decades ago, is now but one task in which communications experts need to have proficiency; crisis communications, internal communications, marketing communications, content creation, social media, multimedia, and speechwriting are several functions (though not all) the modern P.I.O. must become proficient at in order to be successful in today's world of almost instant media access.

Inevitably, for the P.I.O. public relations remains rooted in media relations. To implement strategy in one is to have an understanding of the other. And it is imperative to have an understanding of exactly where our current "media" came from and how they came to be at all if we are to understand the role they play in a proper public relations/media relations strategy. The media we know and love (or love to hate, depending on your leanings and sensibilities) has evolved from its infancy of the screaming of medieval town criers to its current incessant roaring or mewling (again depending on your leanings and sensibilities) through our modern electronic devices. It is a massively intrusive technological monstrosity born of the simplest of ideas: the free sharing of knowledge with all.

But where did such an idea come from? How did it grow and become the force it is today? And what role does it play in your individual view of the world? But also, how does it feed the beast of public opinion with regard to you and your organization? To understand that let us delve into the evolution of media from its earliest of days.

"The advancement and diffusion of knowledge
is the only guardian of true liberty."

-James Madison

A.

Understanding The Role Of News Media: The Power of Knowledge In Recorded History

"Knowledge will forever govern ignorance; and a people who mean to be their own governors must arm themselves with the power which knowledge gives." - James Madison

Throughout history, the possession of information and knowledge has been the scepter of the privileged. While wealth and station have their own merits, it's the mastery of knowledge and the artful deployment of information that has allowed the elite to maintain their dominance. The potency of information is unparalleled. It's the very essence that has enabled the mighty to reign over the meek, ensuring their dominion over the uninformed. Some might even argue, with a hint of cynicism, that this dance of power and manipulation continues to this day.

As the tapestry of history unfurled into the Middle Ages, medieval Europe witnessed the crystallization of distinct societal classes. The

Nobility, draped in opulence and prestige, weren't just mere participants in the grand theater of society; they were its directors. Their dominion over the masses was almost unchallenged by the time the Middle Ages reached its zenith.

But how did this knowledge, this power, proliferate during the Middle Ages to keep even the most downtrodden in check? The answer lies in the sanctified halls of religion. Regardless of personal beliefs, the Clergy emerged as the gatekeepers of information for the masses. By endorsing the Nobility as the divine rulers on Earth, the Clergy fortified the societal hierarchy that had become deeply entrenched in the Middle Ages.

Then there were the Commons, the unsung heroes of society. Not of noble birth, yet possessing a certain gravitas due to their skills or business prowess, they played a pivotal role in the governance and prosperity of the realm. While they might not have been on an equal footing with the Nobility or Clergy, their significance was undeniable.

This is, of course, a bird's eye view of the intricate tapestry of societal classes. It's not an exhaustive historical account, but a primer to set the stage for the birth of a force that would change the course of history: the Media.

From the murmurs of the marginalized emerged an unofficial class, the Fourth Estate. This voice of the common man, amplified through public discourse, began to shape the destiny of nations in ways previously unimagined. History is replete with tales of rulers who underestimated this voice, like Louis XVI and King George III, only to face revolutions that reshaped the world.

The 19th century heralded the formal recognition of this voice as the Press, thanks in no small part to the invention of the printing press. The once-muted whispers of the masses found their voice in leaflets, newsletters, and newspapers. The framers of the Constitution, recognizing the might of this newfound power, enshrined its freedom in the very first amendment, underscoring its pivotal role in the fledgling republic.

By the 1800s, the term 'Fourth Estate' became synonymous with the Press, a beacon for the masses and an indomitable force in the political, economic, and social fabric of nations worldwide.

The Evolution of News Media: From Ink to Internet

"The medium is the message." - Marshall McLuhan

The annals of history are replete with inventions that have reshaped societies, but few have been as transformative as the printing press in the mid-15th century. Before its inception, knowledge was a treasure locked in handwritten manuscripts, accessible only to the privileged few. The printing press democratized information, sowing the seeds for a revolution in literacy and the dissemination of knowledge.

Fast forward to the 16th and 17th centuries, and the printed book reigned supreme. Newspapers, with their tantalizing mix of news and opinion, began to emerge, challenging the status quo. These fledgling publications, often the brainchild of small teams, faced the ever-looming shadow of government censorship. Yet, they persisted.

The 18th and 19th centuries witnessed a technological renaissance. The industrial revolution birthed steam-powered printing presses, amplifying the voice of the press. The telegraph, a marvel of its time, made news dissemination almost instantaneous. Organizations like the Associated Press emerged, casting their net wider to capture news from every corner.

By the dawn of the 20th century, newspapers had woven themselves into the very fabric of daily life. They weren't just sources of information; they were the pulse of society, shaping public opinion. But as the century progressed, new challengers entered the arena: radio and television. While they vied for the same audience, newspapers held their ground, at least for a time.

The 21st century, however, brought with it a digital storm. The internet and social media, those twin titans of the modern age, have reshaped the media landscape. Traditional newspapers, once the sentinels of truth, grapple with this new reality. Yet, amidst the challenges, many have found new life in the digital realm, adapting and evolving.

Radio, too, has undergone its metamorphosis. From the early days of brief bulletins, it has blossomed into a medium rich in content and diversity. The once-formal and authoritative tone has given way to a more conversational, engaging style, drawing in younger, diverse audiences. Digital tools and the omnipresent internet have further revolutionized radio, making it accessible anytime, anywhere.

Television's journey mirrors that of its counterparts. From its humble beginnings, where a single anchor delivered headlines, it has transformed into a multifaceted medium. Today, news is a blend of live reports, expert panels, and in-depth interviews, enhanced by cutting-edge graphics and animations. Yet, it's not just about the format; the content too has diversified, reflecting the myriad interests of a global audience.

But with great power comes great responsibility. The rise of the internet and social media has brought with it the specter of fake news. The ease with which information, or misinformation, can be disseminated poses challenges to public discourse and the very fabric of democracy.

In this ever-evolving tapestry of news media, one thing remains constant: the undying quest to inform and educate. As we stand at the crossroads of tradition and innovation, it's clear that the journey of news media, from ink to internet, is a testament to humanity's insatiable thirst for knowledge.

Much like the growth of a tree, the news media's evolution is rooted in traditional print journalism and has branched out into various platforms, each with its unique set of leaves, representing the diverse ways we now consume news.

<u>Reporters and the Art of Unraveling the "5W's and H"</u>

"The first duty of a newspaper is to be accurate. If it is accurate, it follows that it is fair." - Herbert Bayard Swope

In the intricate dance of journalism, the "5W's and H" serve as the foundational steps. These questions – who, what, where, when, why, and how – are the pillars that uphold the edifice of any compelling news story, providing readers with a comprehensive understanding of the events unfolding before them.

Who: The heart of any narrative. Identifying the key players in a story not only humanizes it but also offers readers a lens through which they can relate. Be it the victims of a natural calamity or the proponents and opponents of a new policy, understanding the "who" paints a vivid picture of the story's impact on individuals and communities.

What: The very essence of the event. This element delves into the core of the incident, providing readers with the specifics. Whether it's the intricacies of a groundbreaking scientific discovery or the details of a new economic policy, the "what" ensures readers grasp the story's significance.

Where: The backdrop against which events unfold. The location sets the stage, offering readers a sense of scale and context. From the epicenter of a natural disaster to the venue of a political rally, the "where" anchors the narrative in a tangible setting.

When: The temporal framework. This element situates the event in time, offering readers a chronological perspective. Whether it's the immediacy of a breaking news event or the historical context of a long-standing issue, the "when" provides a timeline that aids comprehension.

Why: The driving force behind the event. Delving into motivations and underlying causes, the "why" offers readers a deeper insight into the story, allowing them to discern the broader implications and potential ramifications.

How: The mechanics of the event. This element dissects the processes and methods, offering readers a behind-the-scenes look into the unfolding narrative. From the methodology of a groundbreaking research study to the implementation of a new policy, the "how" demystifies complex processes.

Yet, beyond these foundational questions lies an unwavering principle for any public agency spokesperson: honesty. In the delicate balance of public trust, transparency is paramount. A spokesperson stands as the bridge between the agency and the public, and any deviation from the truth can fracture this bond. Misinformation, whether intentional or not, can jeopardize public safety, erode trust, and tarnish an agency's reputation. In an era where credibility is both fragile and invaluable, honesty remains the cornerstone of effective communication.

Think of it like this: Being honest with reporters is like building a house on a solid foundation. It ensures stability, longevity, and trust even in the harshest of weather; whereas dishonesty is like building on sand, which inevitably will shift and collapse especially in the midst of a storm.

B.
Identify and Create Your Image

<u>The Power of Branding in Public Safety</u>

Branding is the art of crafting a distinct identity for an entity, be it a company, product, or even a public safety agency. It's about creating a consistent narrative and visual cue that encapsulates the essence, values, and offerings of the organization. For public safety agencies, branding is not just about recognition; it's about trust, engagement, and community building.

1. Building Trust Through Branding:

A robust brand fosters trust. When the public encounters a cohesive and professional brand from a public safety agency, their confidence in the agency's capabilities grows. This trust is especially vital during emergencies when swift recognition and reliance on the agency can make a significant difference. Moreover, a clear brand narrative can demystify the agency's roles, motivations, and objectives, further solidifying public trust.

2. Enhancing Recognition:

Recognition is a byproduct of consistent branding. In times of crisis, the public can swiftly identify and lean on a well-branded agency. Beyond emergencies, a recognizable brand can amplify public awareness and engagement, ensuring the agency's mission remains at the forefront of community consciousness.

3. Aiding Recruitment:

Branding isn't just outward-facing. A compelling brand narrative can attract potential employees who resonate with the agency's mission and values. It projects professionalism and commitment, making the agency an appealing workplace for those dedicated to public safety.

4. Amplifying Safety Messages:

Branding can be a megaphone for safety campaigns. An agency with a strong brand association can more effectively promote safety messages, ensuring they resonate and stick with the public. This association can drive home the importance of safety protocols, ensuring the public takes proactive steps for their safety.

5. Fostering Public Engagement:

Branding bridges the gap between agencies and the communities they serve. A well-articulated brand fosters a sense of community, making the public more inclined to engage with the agency's initiatives. This engagement can range from participating in community outreach programs to volunteering or even advocating for the agency's mission.

Branding, for public safety agencies, is not just about logos or taglines. It's a comprehensive strategy that fosters trust, enhances recognition, aids recruitment, amplifies safety messages, and fosters public engagement. In essence, it's a tool that ensures the agency's mission resonates, is understood, and is championed by the very community it aims to serve.

Branding for public safety agencies is like a lighthouse on a coast. It serves as a beacon, guiding public perception and ensuring that the agency's mission and values are clearly seen amidst a vast sea of information.

<u>Crafting a Brand Voice</u>

A brand voice is more than just words; it's the embodiment of a brand's ethos, values, and personality. It's the consistent tone and style that a brand uses to communicate across various platforms, from advertisements to social media. For public safety agencies, this voice is pivotal in establishing trust, recognition, and engagement.

Why is a Brand Voice Essential?

1. Audience Resonance: Tailoring your voice to your target audience ensures that your messages resonate. A younger demographic might prefer a more informal tone, while older audiences might lean towards formality. By understanding and addressing these nuances, public safety agencies can foster trust and understanding.

2. Reflecting Brand Personality: Your voice should mirror your brand's character. A playful brand might adopt a light-hearted tone, while one emphasizing transparency might opt for straightforward communication.

3. Upholding Brand Values: Your voice should echo your core values. If your agency prioritizes honesty, your communication should be direct and transparent.

4. Achieving Communication Goals: Your voice should align with your communication objectives. If you aim to be an industry authority, your tone might be more professional and informative.

5. Consistency is Key: A uniform voice across all platforms reinforces brand identity, making it easily recognizable and trustworthy.

Benefits for Public Safety Agencies:

1. Building Trust: A consistent and relatable voice fosters trust. When the public perceives an agency as professional and consistent, they're more likely to rely on it during emergencies.

2. Enhancing Recognition: A distinctive voice helps the public quickly identify and remember the agency, crucial during emergencies.

3. Supporting Recruitment: A strong brand voice can attract potential employees who align with the agency's values.

4. Promoting Safety Messages: A consistent voice amplifies safety campaigns, ensuring the public pays attention and acts accordingly.

5. Boosting Public Engagement: A relatable voice encourages public participation in safety initiatives, fostering a collaborative approach to community safety.

Consistency in Brand Voice:

Consistency in brand voice is paramount. It not only builds brand recognition but also fosters trust. When the public encounters a consistent message, whether on social media or in an advertisement, they're more likely to remember and trust the agency. This consistency:

- Enhances brand recognition.

- Solidifies trust and credibility.

- Strengthens emotional connections with the audience.

- Reinforces brand values.

- Amplifies marketing efforts.

Essentially, for public safety agencies, a consistent and well-crafted brand voice isn't just about branding; it's about building a bond with the community, promoting safety, and ensuring that when the need arises, the public knows who to turn to.

<u>Leveraging Community Partnerships for Public Safety</u>

Community partnerships play a pivotal role in enhancing the public image of safety agencies. By forging alliances with community entities, these agencies can amplify their outreach and foster a collaborative environment to bolster public safety. Here's how these partnerships can elevate the public image of safety agencies:

1. Building Trust Through Collaboration:

   - Partnering with community entities showcases an agency's commitment to collective safety efforts, fostering trust.

   - Collaborative endeavors with respected community groups can bolster an agency's credibility, leveraging the trust these groups have cultivated.

2. Amplifying Visibility:

- Collaborations offer safety agencies a broader platform, enhancing their outreach.

- Joint events or initiatives can garner more attention, spotlighting the agency's efforts.

- Collaborative social media campaigns can tap into larger audiences, further boosting visibility.

3. Credibility Enhancement:

- Tapping into the expertise of community groups can bolster an agency's credibility.

- Joint problem-solving initiatives showcase an agency's commitment to community-centric solutions.

- Public acknowledgment of partnerships underscores an agency's collaborative spirit, further enhancing its credibility.

4. Incorporating Diverse Insights:

- Collaborations foster inclusivity, allowing agencies to benefit from varied perspectives.

- Feedback from community partnerships can offer invaluable insights, ensuring the agency's initiatives resonate with the community.

- Co-created solutions, developed in tandem with community entities, can be more effective and community-centric.

5. Joint Initiatives for Greater Impact:

- Collaborative planning ensures initiatives are tailored to community needs.

- Coordinated efforts between agencies and community groups can lead to more cohesive and impactful initiatives.

- Sharing resources can amplify the impact of safety programs, while community-owned initiatives ensure they resonate with the public.

In effect, community partnerships are invaluable for public safety agencies aiming to enhance their public image. Through trust-building, increased visibility, credibility enhancement, diverse insights, and impactful joint initiatives, these collaborations can significantly elevate the public's perception of safety agencies.

<u>The Influence of Media on Public Perception</u>

Public safety agencies bear the crucial task of conveying vital information to the communities they serve. To do this effectively, they should perceive the news media as a channel to their primary audience, the public, rather than viewing the media as the main audience itself.

Several factors underscore the importance of this perspective:

1. Broad Outreach: The media offers an expansive platform, crucial for rapid information dissemination, especially during emergencies where timely updates can be life-saving.

2. Credibility Boost: Collaborating with esteemed media outlets can lend credibility to the information shared by public safety

agencies. This trust-building is pivotal for ensuring the public acts upon the shared information.

3. Leveraging Expertise: Journalists possess the skills to articulate complex information accessibly. Partnering with the media ensures that public safety messages are clear and comprehensible.

Conversely, if agencies view the media as their primary audience, they might prioritize image management over the content's essence. This can detract from their primary mission: clear and transparent public communication.

Primarily, for public safety agencies, the media should be a bridge to the public. This ensures swift information dissemination, credibility enhancement, and effective message delivery.

In times of crises, public safety agencies are

under the media microscope. While the instinct might be to control the narrative, it's more beneficial to manage the message itself. Here's why:

1. Uncontrollable Media: The media operates independently. In crises, they report unfolding events. Attempts to control them might appear defensive, potentially damaging the agency's reputation.

2. Reputation Risks: Over-defensiveness or perceived secrecy can erode public trust, diminishing the agency's credibility.

3. Trust Building: Transparent communication fosters public trust. This not only enhances the agency's image but ensures the public heeds their advice.

4. Coordinated Response: A focus on message clarity ensures the public receives consistent,

accurate information, aiding a unified crisis response.

Prioritizing message management over media control helps public safety agencies maintain trust, credibility, and effective public communication during crises.

The media's role in shaping public perception is twofold: it reflects and influences public sentiment. This dual function is evident in:

1. Reflecting Public Sentiment: Media outlets often cover topics already resonating with the public, acting as a reflection of prevailing public opinions.

2. Issue Framing: The media's portrayal of events can shape public perceptions. A negative framing can lead to adverse public opinions and vice versa.

3. Agenda Setting: By choosing which stories to highlight, the media can steer public attention, influencing which issues the public deems significant.

4. Information Dissemination: Investigative journalism, for instance, can unveil previously unknown information, reshaping public opinions on specific issues or individuals.

In sum, the media serves as both a mirror and a mold for public opinion, playing an instrumental role in shaping societal views on various topics.

News media's influence on public opinion is like a painter's brush on a canvas. It can shape, color, and define the picture the public sees.

<u>Embedding Your Image in Every Interaction</u>

For public safety agencies, consistently projecting a positive image in every interaction is paramount. Here's how they can seamlessly weave their image into all communications with the public:

1. Unified Branding: Adopting a uniform visual identity, including a recognizable logo, consistent color palette, and specific typography, ensures that the agency is easily identifiable across all communication platforms.

2. Direct Communication: Messages should be straightforward, centered on the agency's core mission and values, and underscore the significance of public safety. This clarity not only informs but also builds trust.

3. Uphold Professional Standards: Maintaining

professionalism in all communications solidifies the agency's reputation as a dependable and authoritative information source. This means clear language, avoiding overly technical terms, and ensuring information is accessible and easy to digest.

4. Engage with Compelling Content: Building a rapport with the public involves sharing relevant and engaging content. Utilizing social media for updates, crafting informative materials on safety topics, and organizing community events can foster a deeper connection between the agency and its audience.

5. Foster Positive Exchanges: Every interaction, whether it's a response to a query or assistance during emergencies, should be approached with respect and promptness. These positive exchanges bolster the agency's image and trustworthiness.

6. Forge Collaborative Alliances: Building strategic relationships with other entities can amplify the agency's reach and image. Collaborations can range from teaming up with local businesses on safety drives, joining forces with other agencies for combined initiatives, or working alongside community organizations to heighten safety awareness.

Effectively, consistently embedding the agency's image in every interaction is pivotal for establishing trust, credibility, and fostering a community-centric approach. Through unified branding, direct communication, professional standards, engaging content, positive exchanges, and collaborative alliances, public safety agencies can fortify their image, underscoring their unwavering commitment to the safety and well-being of the community.

<u>Understanding Your Audiences: Internal vs. External</u>

For public safety agencies, understanding and effectively communicating with both internal and external audiences is pivotal. Each audience has its unique needs and perspectives, and tailoring communication strategies for each can significantly impact the agency's image and effectiveness.

Internal Communication: The Backbone of Agency Image

1. Upholding Core Values: Regular internal communication reinforces the agency's core values and mission. This alignment ensures that employees, who are often the first point of contact with the public, embody and convey the agency's ethos accurately.

2. Boosting Employee Morale: Keeping employees in the loop about the agency's vision and achievements fosters a sense of pride and belonging. Engaged employees are more likely to champion the agency's image and values in their interactions with the public.

3. Consistency is Key: Regular internal briefings ensure that all team members are on the same page, promoting a unified agency image to the public.

4. Building Trust Within: Open channels of communication within the agency foster trust among employees. When staff feel informed and valued, they're more likely to align with the agency's broader goals.

5. Encouraging Constructive Feedback: Open dialogue within the agency can lead to valuable insights. Employees, with their on-the-ground experience, can offer feedback that helps refine the agency's public image and strategies.

Consistently communicating your agency's image internally is like watering a garden. It nurtures growth, unity, and ensures that every plant (or employee) understands its role and purpose.

<u>External Communication: Crafting Public Perception</u>

1. Cultivating Trust: Regularly updating the public on the agency's activities and achievements fosters trust. When communities believe in the agency's capabilities, they're more likely to collaborate and adhere to safety protocols.

2. Building Authority: Consistent and accurate communication positions the agency as a credible source of information. This credibility can enhance public trust and cooperation.

3. Shaping a Positive Image: An active communication strategy helps in molding a favorable public perception. Positive interactions and transparent communication can bolster community support.

4. Championing Openness: Public safety

agencies have a duty to their communities. Regular updates and open channels for feedback emphasize the agency's commitment to transparency and accountability.

5. Educating and Informing: Proactive communication helps in disseminating vital safety information. By keeping the public informed about potential risks and safety measures, agencies can proactively mitigate hazards.

Communicating externally is like a shop window display. It's the first impression the public gets, and it needs to accurately represent what's inside.

In conclusion, for public safety agencies, effective communication isn't just about broadcasting messages. It's about understanding the unique needs of both internal and external audiences and tailoring strategies to foster trust, engagement, and collaboration.

C.
Social Media

Harnessing Digital Word-of-Mouth: The Social Media Advantage

In today's digital age, public safety agencies can harness the power of social media as a modern "word of mouth" to engage and inform their communities. Here's how social media can be a game-changer for these agencies:

1. Real-time Engagement:

Social media platforms enable agencies to share information instantly. This immediacy is invaluable, especially during emergencies when rapid dissemination of accurate information can be lifesaving.

2. Expansive Outreach:

With millions logging into social media daily, these platforms offer agencies a vast audience. This extensive reach ensures that safety messages and initiatives are seen and heard by a broad spectrum of the community.

3. The Virality Factor:

A single impactful post can spread like wildfire on social media, amplifying the agency's message far beyond its usual audience. This virality can be instrumental in raising awareness about critical safety issues.

4. Interactive Communication:

Unlike traditional media, social media is a two-way street. It allows agencies to not only share information but also to listen, respond, and engage with the community, fostering a sense of collaboration and trust.

5. Strengthening Internal Bonds:

For public safety agencies, internal communication is just as crucial. Regular updates and transparent communication via social media can reinforce the agency's mission and values to its staff, ensuring everyone is aligned in their public interactions.

6. Building Public Trust:

Consistent, transparent, and engaging communication via social media can significantly enhance the trust quotient between the agency and the community. When people see agencies actively sharing, responding, and being accessible, it fosters a sense of reliability.

7. Cost-Effective Promotion:

Compared to traditional advertising, social media offers a more budget-friendly way to promote safety campaigns, reach larger audiences, and gauge the impact of these campaigns through analytics.

8. Humanizing the Agency:

Behind every badge or uniform is a human. Sharing stories, behind-the-scenes glimpses, and personal experiences can humanize public safety personnel, bridging the gap between them and the community.

9. Feedback Loop:

Social media provides an avenue for the public to voice concerns, ask questions, and give feedback. This interaction can offer agencies insights into areas of improvement and community sentiment.

10. Crisis Management:

During emergencies, social media becomes a pivotal tool for agencies to share updates, provide directives, and quell rumors, ensuring the public remains informed and calm.

Fundamentally, for public safety agencies, social media isn't just a tool—it's a powerful ally. By leveraging its capabilities, agencies can foster stronger community ties, enhance safety awareness, and build a reputation of trustworthiness and reliability in the digital age.

<u>The Dual Power of Traffic and Engagement</u>

While consistent social media activity is vital for public safety agencies, it's not just about posting regularly. The real magic happens when these posts stimulate engagement. Here's why both elements are crucial:

1. Building Trust and Rapport: Regular updates on social media platforms allow public safety agencies to foster trust within their communities. When agencies emerge as consistent sources of information, they cement their reputation as dependable entities.

2. Staying Top-of-Mind: Regular posts ensure that the public is always informed about safety concerns, emergencies, and other pertinent details. This constant flow of information ensures that the agency remains at the forefront of the community's mind.

3. Fostering Interaction: Regular posting isn't just about broadcasting; it's also about listening. Engaging with comments and feedback shows the community that their voices are heard and valued. This two-way communication strengthens community ties.

4. Amplifying Reach: The more an agency posts and engages, the more visibility they gain. In times of emergencies, this amplified reach can be invaluable for disseminating critical information swiftly.

5. Showcasing the Human Side: Through consistent posts, especially those that offer a glimpse behind the scenes, agencies can humanize themselves. Sharing stories of officers or showcasing daily operations can bridge the gap between the agency and the community.

Consistency in posting lays the foundation, but engagement is the key to truly unlocking the potential of social media for public safety agencies. Here's why engagement is the linchpin:

1. Deepening Connections: Engaging on social media isn't just about responding; it's about connecting. Every interaction is an opportunity for public safety agencies to fortify their relationship with community members.

2. Clarifying and Informing: Direct engagement allows agencies to address questions, clear up misconceptions, and provide additional context. This proactive approach can prevent misinformation from spreading.

3. Boosting Visibility: Active engagement can elevate the agency's posts in social media algorithms, ensuring that their messages reach a broader audience.

4. Tailoring Communication: By actively engaging, agencies can gauge community sentiment, concerns, and needs. This feedback loop can inform future communication strategies, ensuring they remain relevant and effective.

5. Cementing Trust: Timely and respectful responses can underscore an agency's commitment to transparency and accountability, further solidifying public trust.

Principally, while traffic (consistent posting) might be the king of social media for public safety agencies, engagement is undoubtedly the queen. Both are integral for agencies aiming to maximize their impact and foster a safe, informed, and connected community.

Leveraging social media is like harnessing the wind for sailing. Used correctly, it can propel an agency forward, reaching vast audiences and navigating through the vast ocean of public opinion.

<u>Bridging Social Media and Traditional Media</u>

The synergy between social media and traditional media can amplify the reach of public safety agencies. Here's how a robust social media presence can influence and complement traditional media coverage:

1. Amplified Visibility: Regular and engaging posts on social media platforms enhance the visibility of public safety agencies. As their digital footprint grows, traditional media outlets are more likely to notice and feature their content.

2. Spotlight on Noteworthy Content: Sharing compelling stories or groundbreaking initiatives on social media can pique the interest of traditional media. Whether it's a dramatic rescue captured on video or a unique approach to community policing, such content can easily transition from a tweet or post to a news headline.

3. Tapping into Digital Trends: Traditional media often keep a pulse on trending topics and discussions on social media. If content from a public safety agency goes viral or sparks significant online conversation, it's likely to gain traction in conventional news channels.

4. Fostering Media Relations: Interacting with journalists and media houses on social media can cultivate beneficial relationships. A journalist who follows an agency's social media might be inspired by consistent, valuable content, leading to more in-depth features or interviews in mainstream media.

Basically, a strong social media strategy can serve as a catalyst for enhanced coverage in traditional media. By seamlessly integrating the two, public safety agencies can maximize their outreach, ensuring their messages resonate both online and offline.

<u>Harnessing Trends While Maintaining Authenticity</u>

For public safety agencies, striking a balance between tapping into trending content and preserving their unique identity is crucial. Here's how they can achieve this:

1. Define Your Core Message: Before diving into trends, agencies should have a clear understanding of their core message and values. This foundation ensures that any content they produce, whether it's tapping into a trend or not, aligns with their mission.

2. Stay Updated with Trends: By using tools to monitor trending topics and hashtags, agencies can stay in the loop. This allows them to identify relevant trends that resonate with their audience and mission.

3. Engage with Influencers: Building

relationships with influential figures in the social media space can amplify an agency's reach. By sharing or commenting on content from these tastemakers, agencies can gain visibility while also aligning with trusted voices.

4. Tailor Trends to Your Message: When a trend aligns with an agency's mission, it can be adapted to fit their unique message. For instance, during a popular safety awareness week, agencies can share their own safety tips, adding their unique perspective.

5. Produce Original Content: While tapping into trends, agencies shouldn't forget to produce original content that showcases their unique identity. This could be in the form of educational materials, behind-the-scenes glimpses, or personal stories from team members.

6. Maintain Consistency: Regular and

consistent posting helps in building a recognizable online presence. A content calendar can assist agencies in planning their posts, ensuring a mix of trending and original content.

By intertwining trending content with their unique identity, public safety agencies can remain relevant in the ever-evolving social media landscape while staying true to their mission and values. This approach not only enhances their online presence but also fosters trust and engagement within their community.

Using social media to boost traditional media is like using a magnifying glass to focus sunlight. It intensifies and directs attention to where it's most needed.

Navigating the Landscape of Citizen and Independent Reporters

The rise of social media has empowered citizen and independent reporters, allowing them to share news and events in real-time, bypassing traditional journalistic avenues. Platforms like Twitter, Facebook, Instagram, and YouTube have democratized the news-making process, enabling everyday individuals and independent professionals to report and share their narratives.

Citizen reporters, often without formal journalistic training, utilize social media to chronicle events and voice their personal experiences and viewpoints. They frequently shed light on local happenings, from community gatherings to protests, which might go unnoticed by mainstream media. Conversely, independent reporters are seasoned journalists who, having stepped away from conventional news outlets, now independently cover events, often leveraging social media to disseminate their stories and engage with their followers.

For public safety entities, such as police units and emergency response teams, this evolving media landscape presents both opportunities and challenges. While these reporters can offer invaluable on-the-ground insights and real-time updates, the decentralized nature of social media also poses the risk of misinformation spreading rapidly.

To adeptly navigate this environment, public safety agencies should:

1. Develop Clear Engagement Protocols: Establish guidelines on how to interact with citizen and independent reporters on social media platforms.

2. Stay Informed: Actively monitor social media channels to stay updated on unfolding events and to gauge public sentiment.

3. Prioritize Accuracy: In the face of potential misinformation, agencies must prioritize sharing accurate and timely information with the public.

4. Open Direct Communication Lines: Utilize social media to directly communicate with the public and reporters, offering updates, addressing concerns, and answering queries.

In this age of digital democratization, where news-making is no longer the sole domain of traditional media, public safety agencies must adapt and learn to effectively engage with the new wave of citizen and independent reporters. By doing so, they can ensure that accurate information prevails and that the public remains well-informed and safe.

<u>The Digital Image Blueprint</u>

In today's digital age, social media stands as a pivotal platform for public safety agencies to craft and project their image. Platforms like Facebook, Twitter, Instagram, and YouTube offer these agencies a direct line to their communities, allowing them to showcase their values, accomplishments, and dedication in real-time.

Here's how social media can be instrumental in shaping the image of public safety agencies:

1. Bringing a Personal Touch: Through social media, agencies can share narratives about their team members, their day-to-day operations, and their successes. This not only humanizes the agency but also fosters a deeper connection and trust with the community.

2. Championing Openness: By regularly

updating the public about their initiatives, actions, and even challenges, agencies can cultivate a culture of transparency. Addressing public queries and concerns further solidifies this trust.

3. Celebrating Community Ties: By highlighting their participation in community events, outreach programs, or even simple acts of service, agencies can underscore their commitment to the community's well-being, painting a positive and involved image.

4. Demonstrating Expertise: Sharing insightful, well-crafted content can position public safety agencies as authorities in their domain. This not only builds their reputation but also assures the public of their competence and dedication.

5. Broadening Horizons: Social media's vast reach ensures that agencies can connect with a diverse audience, including those who might be unfamiliar with their work. This expanded

visibility can foster greater awareness and appreciation for their role and efforts.

In essence, social media offers public safety agencies a dynamic canvas to paint their story, emphasizing their dedication, professionalism, and community spirit. By harnessing its potential, these agencies can sculpt a trustworthy and commendable digital image.

<u>Harnessing the Power of Top Social Media Platforms</u>

Public safety agencies can harness the vast potential of social media platforms to enhance their operations and foster community relations. Here's how they can leverage the major platforms:

Facebook: The Community Connector

- Direct Communication: Facebook offers a direct line to the community, allowing agencies to share vital updates, address concerns, and highlight their initiatives.

- Emergency Alerts: In times of crisis, Facebook can be instrumental in broadcasting emergency alerts, ensuring the community stays informed.

- Community Engagement: Hosting live sessions, sharing event photos, or spotlighting community partnerships can foster a sense of unity and trust.

- Crime Prevention Tips: Sharing safety guidelines and crime prevention measures can empower the community.

- Recruitment Drive: Highlighting the benefits of joining the force and sharing job postings can attract potential candidates.

Instagram: The Visual Storyteller

- Showcasing Daily Operations: Through photos and short videos, agencies can offer a glimpse into their daily operations, humanizing their force.

- Engaging the Youth: With its younger demographic, Instagram is ideal for connecting with younger community members.

- Collaborating with Influencers: Partnering with local influencers can amplify the agency's reach and message.

Twitter: The Real-time Informer
- Instant Updates: Twitter's real-time nature makes it perfect for sharing on-the-spot

updates, especially during emergencies.

- Engaging in Conversations: Engaging with community members, addressing concerns, or joining trending topics can foster a sense of openness.

- Monitoring Public Sentiment: Tracking hashtags and mentions can provide insights into public sentiment and areas of concern.

YouTube: The Multimedia Educator

- Educational Content: Agencies can share detailed videos on safety protocols, crime prevention tips, or community outreach programs.

- Behind-the-scenes: Offering a peek into training sessions, day-in-the-life videos, or interviews can humanize the force and build trust.

- Community Testimonials: Featuring community members sharing positive interactions or testimonials can foster goodwill.

Content Types and Their Strengths

- Text: Ideal for detailed information, announcements, or sharing stories. Platforms like Twitter and LinkedIn are text-friendly.

- Pictures: Perfect for visual storytelling, showcasing events, or highlighting team members. Instagram and Pinterest thrive on visual content.

- Video: Suited for in-depth content, storytelling, or tutorials. YouTube is the go-to, but Instagram and Facebook also support video content effectively.

Substantially, each platform offers unique strengths. Public safety agencies can craft their content to align with these strengths, ensuring effective communication and fostering a positive community relationship.

D.

Crisis Communication

Navigating Crisis Communication

Crisis—

A period or event marked by instability or high uncertainty, often leading to significant change, with potential negative outcomes.

For public safety agencies, having a robust communication strategy during crises is paramount. This strategy ensures prompt, accurate, and synchronized communication with all relevant parties. Here's why such a plan is indispensable:

1. Prompt Updates: Rapid and effective communication is essential during emergencies. A structured communication plan ensures that vital information reaches stakeholders, such as emergency responders, officials, media, and the general public, without delay.

2. Reliable Information: In the age of rapid information dissemination, misinformation can spread like wildfire. A solid communication strategy ensures that the public receives accurate and consistent updates, preventing panic and confusion.

3. Unified Response: A crisis often involves multiple entities working in tandem. A communication plan ensures that all these entities are aligned in their messaging, promoting a coordinated and efficient response.

4. Reputation Preservation: How an agency communicates during a crisis can significantly impact its public image. Clear and consistent communication can bolster the agency's reputation, portraying it as responsible and responsive.

In effect, during crises, a well-structured communication plan is vital for timely, accurate, and coordinated messaging, which can mitigate damage and potentially save lives.

A public safety crisis typically evolves through several phases, each presenting unique challenges:

1. Initial Shock: Crises often begin unexpectedly, causing initial surprise and urgency.

2. Information Vacuum: Early stages of a crisis might be marked by a lack of complete information, leading to uncertainty and potential missteps.

3. Event Escalation: If not addressed promptly, the situation might worsen, increasing anxiety and necessitating urgent interventions.

4. Feeling Besieged: As the crisis lingers, affected individuals might feel overwhelmed or

trapped, complicating management efforts.

5. Intense Examination: Media and public scrutiny intensify, potentially affecting the perceived effectiveness of the response.

6. Control Erosion: A prolonged crisis might give a sense of diminishing control, challenging the responders.

7. Immediate Focus: The urgency often leads to a narrow focus on immediate resolution, potentially sidelining long-term considerations.

Recognizing these stages can guide emergency responders in crafting effective strategies.

During crises, it's crucial to discern reliable information sources from potential misinformation spreaders. Some questionable sources include:

- Social Media Rumors: While a valuable tool, social media can also propagate unverified information.

- Conspiracy Enthusiasts: These individuals might spread baseless theories, muddying the waters of genuine information.

- Political Opportunists: Some might exploit the crisis for political gains rather than genuine public service.

- Scammers: Taking advantage of the chaos, some might engage in fraudulent activities, like fake charity drives.

- Attention Seekers: Individuals might exaggerate or fabricate stories for personal recognition.

To counteract misinformation, it's vital to rely on verified, trustworthy sources.

During crises, the media often turns to several authoritative sources for updates:

1. Law Enforcement: Police and related agencies are primary sources for updates on situations like active threats or disasters.

2. Emergency Management Bodies: These entities coordinate disaster responses and often collaborate with law enforcement for public updates.

3. Government Representatives: Officials, from city mayors to national leaders, might provide insights and directives during crises.

4. Health Organizations: In health-related emergencies, entities like the CDC or WHO become primary information sources.

5. Medical Responders: In events with casualties, hospitals and emergency medical

teams provide vital updates.

6. Community Pillars: During crises, local leaders or NGOs (non-governmental organizations) involved in relief might also offer valuable insights.

Understanding these sources ensures that the public and media receive accurate and timely information during emergencies.

Effective Crisis Communication

Understanding the Crisis:

A crisis can be defined as a volatile situation with potential negative outcomes. For public safety agencies, having a robust communication strategy during such times is paramount. Here's why:

- Swift Updates: During emergencies, providing prompt updates can prevent panic and confusion. A well-structured communication plan ensures that vital information reaches the public without delay.

- Reliable Information: In the age of misinformation, it's essential to ensure that the data shared is accurate. A communication plan guarantees that the public receives trustworthy information, reducing the spread of rumors.

- Unified Response: Crises often involve

multiple entities. A communication plan ensures that all stakeholders present a coordinated response, avoiding mixed messages.

- Preserving Reputation: How an agency communicates during a crisis can impact its public image. A clear communication strategy can help in maintaining the agency's credibility.

Stages of a Crisis:

1. Initial Shock: The sudden onset of a crisis can lead to widespread surprise and panic.

2. Information Void: Early stages of a crisis might have limited information, leading to uncertainty.

3. Escalating Situation: If not managed, the crisis can intensify, causing more panic.

4. Feeling Trapped: Prolonged crises can lead to a sense of helplessness among the public.

5. Public Scrutiny: The media and public will

closely monitor the situation, often critically.

6. Feeling Overwhelmed: As the crisis continues, there might be feelings of losing control.

7. Immediate Response Mode: The focus becomes resolving the current situation, often neglecting long-term implications.

Trustworthy vs. Untrustworthy Information:

During crises, misinformation can arise from various sources, including social media, conspiracy theorists, opportunistic politicians, scammers, and attention-seekers. It's crucial to rely on verified sources for accurate updates.

On the other hand, reliable information typically comes from law enforcement agencies, emergency management bodies, government officials, public health organizations, emergency medical services, and community leaders.

Crafting the Right Message:

1. Prioritize Information: Ensure that the public knows about available resources, which can provide reassurance, foster cooperation, enhance trust, and aid decision-making.

2. Involve Spokespersons: Having a spokesperson at high-level meetings ensures that the public receives timely, consistent, and credible information, shaping positive public perception.

3. Identify the Audience: Different groups, including the general public, first responders, policymakers, and partner organizations, need tailored information.

4. Timeliness Matters: Providing accurate information promptly can ensure public safety, reduce panic, foster trust, and promote inter-agency cooperation.

Positive Communication:

Using uplifting language during crises can calm nerves, foster trust, motivate action, and clarify information. Initial statements should exude care and concern, establishing empathy, showcasing responsibility, offering emotional support, and preventing backlash.

Action-Oriented Communication:

It's essential to inform the public about the steps being taken during a crisis. This transparency can reassure the public, manage expectations, inspire hope, and foster trust.

Message Hierarchy:

When conveying a message during a crisis, prioritize in this order:

- People/Pets: Emphasize immediate safety measures for individuals and their pets.

- Environment: Address any environmental concerns or hazards.

- Property: While significant, property concerns should come after ensuring the safety of people and the environment.

By focusing on these elements, public safety agencies can ensure that their crisis communication is effective, timely, and prioritizes the well-being of the community.

<u>Why a Communication Plan is Essential</u>

In times of crisis, swift and clear communication is paramount. Here's why public safety agencies should have a crisis communication blueprint:

- Swift Response: Crises are time-sensitive. A ready-to-deploy communication plan ensures immediate and efficient action, eliminating the scramble to strategize amidst chaos.

- Unified Messaging: A plan ensures consistent messaging across all communication platforms, reducing potential misinformation and confusion.

- Trust Maintenance: Timely and accurate information fortifies public trust, assuring them that the situation is under control.

- Readiness: Anticipating potential crises and

having a plan ensures a proactive approach,
reducing potential damages.

- Legal Compliance: Some jurisdictions
mandate crisis communication plans, making it
not just a best practice but a legal necessity.

<u>Roles in Crisis Communication</u>

During emergencies, six key Public Information Officers (PIOs) roles emerge:

1. Lead PIO: Oversees the entire communication strategy, ensuring message coherence and media relationship management.

2. Media Staging Liaison: Coordinates on-site media activities, ensuring journalists have accurate information.

3. Mainstream Media Monitor: Tracks traditional media outlets to ensure accurate reporting.

4. Social Media Monitor: Monitors and engages with online platforms to address concerns and rectify misinformation.

5. Victim Support Liaison: Engages with victims and their families, ensuring they receive timely information and support.

6. Administrative PIO: Handles the bureaucratic side of communication, from

record-keeping to legal compliance.

<u>Cultural and Linguistic Preparedness</u>

Effective crisis communication transcends language and cultural barriers:

- Safety First: Diverse communication ensures everyone, regardless of language or culture, understands risks and safety measures.

- Building Trust: Tailored communication fosters trust, showing responsiveness and responsibility.

- Legal Considerations: Some laws mandate multilingual communication, ensuring everyone is informed.

- Public Image: Effective multicultural communication enhances an agency's reputation, showcasing its inclusivity and sensitivity.

<u>Media Resource Management</u>

In a crisis, various media resources are essential:

- Press Conference Zone: A dedicated space for official statements.

- Media Staging Area: A space for media personnel to gather and relay information.

- Live Broadcasts: Real-time updates, interviews, and briefings.

- Social Media Engagement: Official accounts providing real-time updates and clarifications.

- Media Pool: A system ensuring equal media access when on-site numbers need limiting.

- Satellite Communication: Ensuring uninterrupted communication, especially in remote areas.

- Media Kits: Prepared packages containing vital information about the crisis.

<u>Prioritize Timely Information Release</u>

Being the first to release accurate information during a crisis is crucial:

- Accuracy: As primary information sources, public safety agencies ensure the first wave of information is correct.

- Safety Protocols: Immediate information release ensures the public can promptly take protective actions.

- Message Control: Releasing information first prevents the spread of potential misinformation.

- Trust Building: Timely communication underscores the agency's commitment to public safety.

- Collaborative Response: Ensures all stakeholders are aligned in their response efforts.

<u>Set Clear Goals</u>

In a crisis, clarity is key:

- Clear Objectives: Everyone involved should know their roles, ensuring a unified response.

- Resource Allocation: Clear goals ensure optimal use of limited resources.

- Efficiency: With set goals, efforts are streamlined, avoiding unnecessary diversions.

- Performance Metrics: Clearly defined goals allow for measurable outcomes and adjustments if needed.

- Accountability: With set objectives, everyone's contributions can be evaluated.

Public Communication of Goals

Clearly communicating goals to the public during a crisis is vital:

- Transparency: It shows the agency's commitment to open communication.

- Trust Building: Clear goals show the public that the situation is being managed with a clear strategy.

- Collaboration: It ensures everyone, including the public, is aligned in their response.

- Accountability: Publicly stated goals mean the agency can be held accountable for its actions.

- Public Engagement: Clear goals can inspire public participation in the crisis response.

<u>Understanding Agency Policies and Processes</u>

Public knowledge of agency policies and processes during a crisis is beneficial:

- Transparency: It showcases the agency's commitment to open governance.

- Decision-making Insight: It helps the public understand the rationale behind certain actions.

- Public Preparedness: Knowing agency processes helps the public anticipate and prepare for actions.

- Collaboration: Understanding processes fosters a collaborative spirit between the public and agencies.

- Empowerment: Informed citizens can actively engage with officials, ensuring a more effective response.

Public Communication of Actions

Informing the public about actions taken during a crisis is beneficial:

- Clarity: It helps the public understand the ongoing situation and the agency's response.

- Safety Protocols: It ensures the public knows the necessary safety steps to take.

- Reassurance: It assures the public that the situation is being actively managed.

- Accountability: It holds agencies accountable for their actions.

- Future Preparedness: It helps the public prepare for potential future crises.

Effectively, effective crisis communication is a blend of preparation, clarity, transparency, and timely action. Public safety agencies must prioritize these elements to ensure the safety and trust of the public they serve.

A crisis communication plan is like a lifeboat on a ship. You hope you never need it, but when a storm hits and the ship is going down, it's essential for survival.

E.

The Press Conference

<u>Projecting the Right Image</u>

For public safety agencies, how they present themselves during media briefings can significantly influence public perception. Here's how they can ensure a positive image during press interactions:

1. Embrace Transparency: Always be open about the situation at hand. Sharing relevant details and answering questions honestly fosters trust between the agency and both the media and the public.

2. Maintain Professionalism: A polished appearance matters. Ensure that the spokesperson is appropriately attired, the setting is neat, and the message delivered is clear and well-structured.

3. Incorporate Visuals: Utilizing visual aids like graphs, illustrations, or photographs can

simplify complex information, making it more digestible and engaging for the audience.

4. Showcase Achievements: Highlight the agency's accomplishments, whether they're innovative strategies employed or commendable actions by team members. Sharing positive stories reinforces the agency's competence and dedication.

5. Address and Acknowledge: If there are prevailing concerns or criticisms, address them head-on. This shows the agency's commitment to accountability and continuous improvement.

6. Stay Accessible: Offer avenues for further communication. Providing contact details for follow-up queries or concerns encourages ongoing communication and shows the agency's dedication to public engagement.

Selecting a Relevant Topic

For a press conference to be successful, it's crucial to choose a topic that's current and of significant interest to the public. News agencies prioritize stories that resonate with their audience. Hence, the subject of the press conference should be timely, pertinent, and impactful on a broad scale. A topic that lacks relevance might not garner the desired media attention, making the effort counterproductive.

Meeting Attendee Expectations
==========

To ensure a seamless press conference, it's vital to cater to the attendees' needs:

- Comfort: Offer a conducive environment with appropriate seating, temperature, and refreshments.

- Technical Support: Equip the venue with necessary tools like high-speed internet, AV equipment, and presentation aids.

- Travel and Stay: For out-of-town attendees, provide details about lodging and transportation.

- Information Access: Distribute essential documents, press releases, or research reports related to the conference.

- Safety Protocols: Ensure the venue adheres to safety standards and has emergency plans in place.

Briefing Participants

All individuals involved in the press conference should be well-prepped to:

- Maintain a unified message.

- Adhere to the event's timeline.

- Uphold a professional demeanor.

- Manage unexpected challenges.

- Interact adeptly with the media.

<u>Adapting to Unforeseen News</u>

Press conferences can sometimes be overshadowed by unexpected major news events. Such events can divert media attention, leading to reduced or even no coverage of the scheduled conference. It's essential to:

- Stay Flexible: Be ready to adjust the conference's agenda or focus based on external events.

- Maintain Engagement: Keep the audience's attention even if there's a shift in the broader news landscape.

- Prioritize Relevance: If breaking news directly relates to the hosting agency, it might be necessary to refocus the conference to address the new developments.

Materially, while planning a press conference, it's crucial to select a pertinent topic, cater to attendees' needs, ensure all participants are briefed, and remain adaptable to the ever-changing news environment.

<u>Maintaining a Strong Public Image</u>

When organizing a press conference, understanding the media experience of your speakers is crucial for several reasons:

Clear Messaging: Trained speakers can articulate their points more effectively, ensuring that the core message is conveyed clearly and understood by the audience.

Navigating Tough Questions: Those with media experience are adept at handling challenging questions, ensuring that they remain composed and on-message even under pressure.

Upholding Professional Standards: Experienced speakers are more likely to exude professionalism, understanding the nuances of media interactions and the importance of presenting a positive image.

Attracting Media Attention: A speaker's media experience can be a draw for news outlets, increasing the likelihood of extensive coverage.

Reinforcing Organizational Reputation: A well-executed press conference can bolster an organization's image. Experienced speakers play a pivotal role in ensuring the event enhances the organization's standing.

The Role of Prepared Statements

Consistency: Prepared statements ensure that information relayed is consistent, reducing the risk of miscommunication.

Focused Messaging: These statements guide speakers, ensuring they remain on-topic and avoid potential pitfalls.

Projecting Professionalism: A prepared statement underscores a speaker's professionalism, indicating thorough preparation.

Ensuring Accuracy: Such statements are typically vetted for accuracy, ensuring that all information shared is correct and up-to-date.

Facilitating Media Reporting: Clear, prepared statements make it easier for journalists to report on the event, ensuring accurate media coverage.

The Importance of Post-Conference Interviews

Depth and Detail: One-on-one interviews post-conference allow journalists to delve deeper, asking detailed questions to enhance their coverage.

Efficient Event Management: Knowing which speakers are available for interviews helps in organizing the flow of the event, preventing bottlenecks or confusion.

Timely Execution: Being aware of speakers' availability ensures the event adheres to its schedule, preventing unnecessary delays.

Understanding which speakers are available for individual interviews post-conference is vital. It aids in providing journalists with comprehensive information, ensures smooth event management, and guarantees timely execution of the press conference's agenda.

<u>Engaging the Media</u>

For a successful press conference, it's crucial to effectively engage the media. Here's a guide to ensure the media's attendance and coverage:

1. Advance Planning: Begin preparations early. This allows ample time for refining details and ensuring the media can fit the event into their schedules.

2. Identify Relevant Media: Research and pinpoint the media outlets that align with the press conference's theme. Gather contacts of pertinent reporters and editors.

3. Draft a Media Alert: Craft a succinct media alert detailing the who, what, when, where, and why of the press conference. Aim to send this out a week prior to the event.

4. Personalized Outreach: Beyond the general alert, personally reach out to key media figures. Offer them a deeper insight into the event's significance and why it would be of interest to their audience.

5. Logistics Communication: Clearly

communicate logistical aspects. This includes parking details, registration processes, and any specific media equipment accommodations.

6. Open Channels for Queries: Ensure you're accessible to address any media inquiries leading up to the event. This not only aids in accurate reporting but also fosters a positive rapport with the media.

7. Reminder Alerts: A day or two before the event, send out a reminder. This reinforces the event's importance and keeps it on the media's radar.

By adhering to these steps, organizers can maximize media attendance and ensure comprehensive and accurate event coverage.

<u>Crafting Your Press Kit</u>

A press kit serves as an informational toolkit for journalists, offering a detailed overview of the event or subject in question. Here's a breakdown of the essential components to include in a press kit for a press conference:

1. Official Press Release: This is a structured document detailing the core facts about the press conference. It should outline the who, what, when, where, and why, and may also feature notable quotes from principal speakers or stakeholders.

2. Contextual Details: Dive deeper into the subject of the press conference by providing relevant background. This could encompass related statistics, historical insights, or any pertinent data that enriches the narrative.

3. Profiles of Speakers: Offer brief biographies

of the main speakers, highlighting their professional journey, notable achievements, and any other information that underscores their authority on the topic.

4. Visual Elements: Incorporate images, charts, or infographics that visually represent the subject matter. This might include portraits of the speakers, data visualizations, or other relevant imagery that can enhance a journalist's coverage.

5. Organization Overview: Give a snapshot of the hosting entity, whether it's a company, institution, or another organization. Detail its origin, objectives, and any other salient information that paints a clearer picture for the media.

6. Connectivity Details: Ensure journalists have a straightforward way to reach out for further inquiries. List out phone numbers, email addresses, and even social media profiles

of the event organizers or PR representatives.

Essentially, a well-structured press kit acts as a roadmap for media professionals, guiding them through the event's key points and offering a holistic understanding. By presenting this data in an organized and accessible format, organizers can optimize media coverage and engagement.

Most public safety press conferences are regarding major, ongoing incidents. But occasionally we get to call the media to us for our own purposes. Choosing a newsworthy topic for a press conference is like fishing with the right bait. It ensures you'll catch the attention of the media and the public.

F.
Going On Camera

<u>Optimizing Your Press Conference Venue</u>

The choice of venue for a public safety agency's press conference can significantly influence public perception and the effectiveness of the message conveyed. Here's why the management of the venue is pivotal:

1. Safety First: The primary concern should always be the safety of the spokesperson, media personnel, and attendees. A secure location ensures that the press conference can proceed without interruptions or threats.

2. Reinforcing the Message: The venue can either reinforce or detract from the message. For instance, a calm and organized setting can underscore the agency's control over a situation, while a chaotic backdrop might suggest the opposite.

3. Visual Context: The visual backdrop

provided by the venue can set the tone for the entire press conference. A well-chosen location can enhance the message, while a poorly chosen one can distract or even contradict it.

4. Community Engagement: The proximity of the venue to the incident or affected community can demonstrate the agency's commitment and concern. It shows that the agency is present, involved, and attentive to the community's needs.

5. Practical Considerations: Beyond the message, the venue should be logistically sound. It needs to be accessible for all – from media crews with their equipment to agency representatives and the general public. Adequate space, parking, and facilities can ensure the event runs smoothly.

In substance, the venue for a press conference isn't just a physical location; it's an extension of the message. By meticulously selecting and managing the venue, a public safety agency can ensure its message is clear, credible, and effectively delivered.

Choosing the right location for a press engagement is like setting the stage for a play. The backdrop, lighting, and ambiance all play a role in conveying the story's message.

<u>Crafting a Professional Image On Camera</u>

When representing a public safety agency on camera, the spokesperson's attire plays a pivotal role in shaping public perception. Here's a guide to ensuring a polished and professional image:

Dress Code Essentials:

1. Appropriateness: Tailor your attire to the event's formality. A corporate press release might necessitate a suit, while an on-site emergency briefing could call for a more relaxed yet professional look.

2. Cleanliness: Ensure clothes are spotless, wrinkle-free, and fit well. Ill-fitting or unkempt attire can detract from the message.

3. Color Palette: Stick to neutral shades like black, grey, or navy. These colors exude professionalism and reduce distractions. Avoid overly vibrant colors unless they align with the agency's branding.

4. Accessories: Opt for subtle accessories like watches or ties. Avoid anything too flashy or trendy.

5. Footwear: Shoes should be pristine and polished. Avoid casual footwear like sneakers or sandals.

6. Grooming: Present a well-groomed appearance, from tidy hair and nails to minimal makeup or fragrance.

For Public Safety Spokespersons On-Camera:

1. Functional Attire: Wear clothes that are both comfortable and suitable for the context. This could range from a suit for press conferences to a uniform for on-site briefings.

2. Agency Identification: Always display an official badge or wear a uniform showcasing the agency's emblem. This not only establishes authority but also fosters trust.

3. Footwear: Opt for comfortable yet professional shoes. While men might choose dress shoes, women can select between dress shoes, flats, or modest heels.

4. Personal Grooming: Maintain a neat appearance. This includes well-styled hair and, if applicable, trimmed facial hair. Ensure hands are clean and nails are manicured.

5. Safety Equipment: If the situation demands, like on an emergency site, ensure safety gear such as helmets or vests are worn. They should be clean and fit for purpose.

Basically, when appearing on camera for a public safety agency, it's crucial to strike a balance between being relatable and authoritative. A professional appearance not only enhances the spokesperson's credibility but also reinforces the agency's commitment to public welfare.

Dressing for the camera is like wearing the right outfit for an occasion. It sets the tone, conveys respect for the audience, and ensures the message isn't overshadowed.

<u>Presenting with Confidence: Body Language and Focus</u>

The way a spokesperson presents themselves on camera, from their posture to their gaze, plays a pivotal role in conveying authority and trustworthiness. Here's a guide to mastering these non-verbal cues for effective on-camera communication:

1. Upright Posture: Stand tall with shoulders relaxed but pulled back. This not only exudes confidence but also ensures the spokesperson appears engaged and attentive.

2. Hand Dynamics: Hands can be expressive, but they shouldn't be distracting. Refrain from excessive hand movements or fidgeting. Instead, use them to emphasize points subtly. When not gesturing, keep hands relaxed at the sides or clasped lightly in front.

3. Steady Stance: Position feet about shoulder-width apart for balance. This stance is both comfortable and portrays stability. Avoid unnecessary movements like pacing or shifting from foot to foot, which can come off as nervousness.

4. Engaging Eyes: Maintain consistent eye contact with the camera or interviewer. This establishes a connection with the audience and reinforces sincerity. Avoiding the camera can give an impression of evasion or lack of confidence.

5. Expressive Face: While it's essential to be professional, a warm and approachable facial expression can make the message more relatable. Occasional smiles, when appropriate, can humanize the spokesperson and make them more relatable.

6. Open Body Language: Ensure the body remains open and directed towards the camera

or interviewer. Crossing arms or legs can be perceived as defensive or closed off. Instead, adopt a stance that's receptive and welcoming.

Inherently, the way a spokesperson stands, moves, and looks can significantly influence the audience's perception. By mastering these non-verbal cues, spokespersons can enhance their on-camera presence, ensuring their message is not only heard but also trusted and respected.

Maintaining the right posture and presentation is like a musician tuning their instrument. It ensures that the performance is pitch-perfect and resonates with the audience.

Embrace the Silence

Silence or "dead air" during an on-camera interview refers to those moments when neither the interviewer nor the interviewee is speaking. While it might seem unsettling, these pauses can arise from various reasons, including technical glitches, a natural lull in the conversation, or the interviewer's strategy to elicit more information.

For both the person being interviewed and the interviewer, these silent moments can feel awkward, potentially leading to rushed answers or filler words just to break the silence. However, it's essential to remember that maintaining a steady flow of conversation and having backup questions or topics can help navigate these quiet periods.

In live broadcasts, dead air is especially concerning. It can lead to viewers switching channels or feeling disengaged. Broadcasters often employ strategies to counteract this, such as having an off-camera team ready with prompts, using background music, or cutting to pre-recorded segments during unexpected pauses.

Interestingly, some interviewers intentionally use dead air as a tactic, hoping the interviewee will fill the silence with more information or details. If you're the one being interviewed, it's crucial to remain composed during these moments. If you've adequately addressed a question, there's no need to add more just because of a pause. Embracing the silence can sometimes be more powerful than filling it without purpose.

<u>Navigating "Off the Record" Conversations</u>

"Off the record" is a journalistic term indicating that the provided information should not be publicly reported or attributed to the source. Essentially, it's a confidential sharing of information between the source and the journalist. While this can offer journalists insights they might not otherwise receive, it's a practice that comes with its own set of challenges and considerations.

When someone opts to speak "off the record," they're sharing details they might not be comfortable disclosing publicly. However, it's crucial to distinguish between "off the record" and "not for attribution." The latter means the information can be reported but without directly attributing it to the source. Terms like "on background" or "on deep background" serve similar purposes, and the nuances between them can vary.

Given the varying interpretations and practices surrounding "off the record" across media outlets, both the source and the journalist must establish clear boundaries and understandings before delving into such discussions.

For spokespersons representing public safety agencies, it's typically advised to steer clear of "off the record" remarks to the media due to several reasons:

1. Transparency Commitment: Public safety agencies owe the public a duty of transparency. Sharing information "off the record" can be perceived as a lack of openness or an attempt to control the narrative.

2. Message Consistency: "Off the record" comments can lead to mixed messages, potentially causing public confusion or mistrust.

3. Potential Risks: Such comments can pose risks to the agency. If an "off the record" remark is later deemed misleading or false, it

can tarnish the agency's reputation and even lead to legal repercussions.

4. Ethical Implications for Journalists: Journalists operate under their own set of ethical guidelines. Being privy to "off the record" information can place them in challenging positions, especially if they're torn between withholding vital information and their duty to inform the public.

Mainly, to maintain transparency, uphold consistent messaging, mitigate potential risks, and respect journalistic ethics, public safety agency representatives are generally advised to communicate on the record and avoid "off the record" disclosures.

Speaking 'off the record' is like whispering a secret. It's meant for one person's ears, but there's always a risk it could be overheard.

Always Be Camera-Ready

Public agency representatives should operate under the principle that the camera is always on. This mindset is crucial when engaging with the media, as any statement or gesture can potentially be captured and broadcasted. Here's why adopting this approach is essential:

1. Consistent Messaging: Being perpetually camera-ready ensures that spokespersons consistently convey their intended message. It encourages careful word choice and a consistent tone, ensuring clarity and minimizing misunderstandings.

2. Professionalism: Recognizing that every word could be recorded encourages a high level of professionalism. This not only pertains to verbal communication but also to body language, facial expressions, and overall demeanor.

3. Avoiding Missteps: Offhand remarks or casual comments can sometimes be misconstrued or taken out of context. By always being mindful of the ever-present camera, spokespersons can sidestep potential pitfalls or controversies that could arise from unplanned statements.

4. Upholding Reputation: For public agencies, reputation is paramount. By always being on guard, spokespersons can ensure they uphold and enhance the agency's image, avoiding any negative press that could arise from careless comments.

Effectively, adopting a "camera is always on" mentality is a proactive strategy for public agency spokespersons. It ensures they remain at their best, delivering clear, consistent, and professional communication at all times.

Always assuming the camera is rolling is like a goalkeeper always being ready for a shot. Even if

*the ball is far away, they're alert, knowing it could
come their way any second.*

As we dock our metaphorical ship I invite you to pause and reflect on the voyage we've undertaken together through the vast and sometimes tumultuous seas of public safety communication.

Our journey began by exploring the transformative power of news media, where we acknowledged its capacity to shape and shift the sands of public perception, much like the ocean shapes the shoreline. We recognized that the internet and social media, with their boundless horizons, can be both a gentle breeze that guides us and a formidable storm that challenges our navigation skills.

In the vast ocean of communication, honesty has been our steadfast compass, always pointing us towards true north, ensuring our path remains unswerving and our reputation unsullied. We hoisted our flag of branding high, allowing it to flutter boldly and declare our identity and values to the distant shores and neighboring vessels.

Consistency in our messaging, akin to the rhythmic pulse of our vessel, has been the undercurrent propelling us forward, ensuring our narrative remains coherent and our journey purposeful. We've learned that our social media lookouts are vital, scanning the horizons for emerging trends and potential crises, enabling us to navigate through the digital waves with foresight and agility.

Our communications plan, the meticulously charted map, has been our guide through calm and storm, ensuring that even amidst a tempest of crises, our messages find their harbor. Press conferences, our anchors, have grounded us, providing a stable platform from which to share our tales with the world. Our press kit,

the treasure chest, has been safeguarded, its
contents precious, ready to be unveiled to those
who seek our stories.

We've dressed our crew – the location, attire,
and posture – meticulously, ensuring that every
member plays their part in presenting a united,
professional front. We've learned to navigate
the precarious waters of off-the-record
comments and to always be vigilant, for the
camera is ever-watchful, ever-rolling.

In each chapter of our journey, we've
encountered challenges and revelations, and
it's my hope that these pages have equipped
you with the tools, strategies, and insights to
navigate your own narrative through the vast
sea of public safety communication.

As we anchor our ship at the journey's end,
let's make a pact: to take charge of our

narratives, to be the authors of our own tales, and to navigate our ships with confidence through the ever-shifting seas of media relations. In an era where stories are disseminated at lightning speed across digital waves, it is imperative, now more than ever, for public safety agencies to seize the helm and steer their narratives with authority, authenticity, and transparency.

May our stories, told with honesty and integrity, illuminate the seas of media relations, providing a beacon of truth in the boundless ocean of narratives. Let us sail forth, steadfast, as we write our own headlines, beyond the tempest, into the tranquil seas of understanding and trust.

This book was created and published in conjunction with a weeklong, in-depth media relations training course: Media and Public Relations For Public Safety Professionals. For information on upcoming courses or to schedule training at your agency or organization visit www.delkmediagroup.com.